Quick Thinking

Written by
Rob Waring and **Maurice Jamall**

Before You Read

to drop

to fall

to fly

to swim

beach

car

a cart

lake

plane

police officer

quick

In the story

Faye

David

Tyler

Daniela

John

John and Tyler are in the park. They are showing everybody their cars and planes.
"These are really great!" says Tyler. John talks to his friends Faye and David.
"Faye and David, do you want to try?" asks John.
Faye says, "No thanks, we're going to the beach."
"Do you want to come?" asks David.

"No thanks, David," John says. "Have a good time at the beach."
"Okay, see you later," say David and Faye.
David says, "It's a great day to swim. Come on, Faye."
"Yes, let's go," replies Faye.
John and Tyler play with their cars and planes in the park.

David and Faye go down to the beach. They see their friend Daniela.

"Hi, Daniela, it's hot today!" says Faye.

"Hi. Yeah. Do you want ice cream?" Daniela asks.

Faye says, "Yes, please." David gives her the money.

"We're going swimming," says Faye.

"Okay, have a good time. See you later," says Daniela.

Faye and David walk down onto the beach. They are going swimming.
There are many people on the beach. Some people are walking on the beach. Dogs are playing on the beach, too. Everybody is having a great time.

Faye and David put their things on the beach.
They are getting ready to swim.
They see a man running on the beach.
"David, what's that man doing?" asks Faye.
"I don't know," replies David. "I don't know."
"He's running very fast," says Faye.

The man has a bag.

"Stop! Stop!" shouts a woman. "Stop him! He has my bag."

Faye says, "That man has the woman's bag!"

"Quick, let's stop him," says David.

"But how? Think. Quick, David, think!" says Faye.

The man is running away.

"Where's he going?" asks David.

"He's going to the street, I think," Faye says.

Faye gets her phone. She calls Daniela.

"Daniela, it's Faye. Stop that man, Daniela," she says.

"Okay, but which man?" asks Daniela.

"The man in gray. He has a woman's bag. He's coming to you," says Faye.

"Okay, I can see him," says Daniela. "I'll stop him," she says.

Daniela pushes the cart into the man. The man falls down. He drops the woman's bag.
Daniela tries to stop the man, but she can't. The man is very big and he's too strong. Daniela can't stop him.
The man gets up and takes the woman's bag. He runs away to the park.

Faye and David run to Daniela.

"Are you okay, Daniela?" they ask.

"Yes, I'm okay," she says. "I'm sorry, he's running away.
He's going into the park."

Daniela says, "Let's stop him."

"But how?" asks Faye. "What can we do, David?" she asks.
"Do you have an idea?"

David calls Tyler.

"Tyler, it's David," he says. "Can you see a man running into the park?"

Tyler asks, "Yes. Does he have gray pants and a gray shirt?"

"Yes," says David. "Stop him! He has a woman's bag."

"Okay, we'll stop him. But how?" asks Tyler. "He's a big man. I can't stop him."

"Think!" says David.

Tyler tells John about the man. The man is running through the park with the woman's bag.
"He's running very fast," says John.
Tyler asks, "How can we stop him? He's running too fast."
"I have an idea," says John. "I know! We can stop him!"

"Let's use the cars and planes," says John. John makes his car go to the man. John's car hits the man.
"Good job, John!" says Tyler. Tyler's car hits the man, too. The man is surprised and he falls over. He drops the bag. Tyler and John tell the other boys about the man.

Many people help John and Tyler. They want to stop the man. Their cars and planes fly at the man. Tyler's car hits the man again and again. This time, the man falls into the lake.

"Good job, Tyler!" says John.

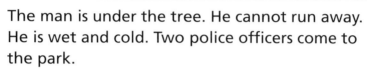

The man is under the tree. He cannot run away. He is wet and cold. Two police officers come to the park.

"Thank you, thank you very much," says a police officer.

Tyler tells him about Faye, David and Daniela, too. "That *is* quick thinking!" he says.